# TODAY MEANS AMEN

*poems*

## SIERRA DeMULDER

Andrews McM
Publishing
a division of Andrews McMeel

Andrews McMeel Publishing
a division of Andrews McMeel Universal
1130 Walnut Street, Kansas City, Missouri 64106

www.andrewsmcmeel.com

16 17 18 19 20 RR4 10 9 8 7 6 5 4 3 2 1

ISBN: 978-1-4494-7411-9

Library of Congress Control Number: 2015950225

Editor: Grace Suh
Art director: Holly Ogden
Production editor: Erika Kuster
Production manager: Carol Coe
Demand planner: Sue Eikos

**ATTENTION: SCHOOLS AND BUSINESSES**
Andrews McMeel books are available at quantity discounts with
bulk purchase for educational, business, or sales promotional use.
For information, please e-mail the Andrews McMeel Publishing
Special Sales Department: specialsales@amuniversal.com.

Cover image © Madeleine Brunnmeier | www.mademoments.de
Author photo by Hillary Olson

The following poems previously appeared in *We Slept Here*, published by
Button Poetry (2015):
 "Uninhabitable"
 "After Googling Affirmations for Abuse Survivors"
 "Release It"

The following poems previously appeared in *New Shoes on a Dead Horse*,
published by Write Bloody Publishing (2012):
 "The Origin of Breast Milk"
 "The Origin of the Bathrobe"

*. . . it is that you're my friend out here on the far reaches*
*of what humans can find out about each other.*

—JASON SHINDER, "CODA"

This book is dedicated to my dear friend Sam.

# contents

## BOWL OF DIAMONDS

## A BEEHIVE PITCHED IN THE RIVER

## PAY THE BOATMAN

## SOME INVISIBLE MACHINE

# SING TO ME THEN

# BOWL OF
# DIAMONDS

## In the In-Between

We finally decided to leave each other.

To throw in the towel as they say, which
makes me think of our love as some

red-faced boxer—lips ballooning, eyes

disappearing inside themselves—or,
as a laboring woman—belly round, heeing

and hawing. Our love trying to push out

new life, and us, two scared nurses, dabbing
away the sweat on her brow or cleaning

the blood from his busted lip. Our love:

not pregnant, nor a good left hook, but
it did put up one hell of a fight. We chose

to forfeit, to finish it. Our love: some

shitty novel or a board game that just
goes on and on forever—*just end it!*

Maybe it's an animal struck down

by a car. I've heard deer make the most
human of noises as they die—*just*

*end it.* The night we did, we slept

the kind of touchless sleep that follows
a funeral. I woke midday to the sound

of stillness, nothing, and knew where

our love lives now. Our bodies
refusing to rouse to a world bled of it.

Some part of us wanted to stay there,

in the in-between, where the baby
isn't stillborn, where the deer runs off

into the meadow, where the boxer

just gets up, punch after punch,
and the rounds go on forever.

## My Lover Found Me Weeping
## on the Couch

reading the obituary of a local father,
not much older than you or I, whose body
betrayed him too soon—or should I say at all,

ever, because what kind of body is so disloyal
as to feed a tumor until it is fat as a blister
inside the skull, a snail too big for its shell—

I couldn't help but think of the boy, his son,
still in that intangible stage between baby
and person, between *magic is real* and *magic*

*is not real because if it was, it would have*
*saved my father.* I wept for him and sneered
at the audacity of death, how it is the boldest

of all things, how it comes and goes as it pleases.
And once I was done, once everything was dry
and dull again, my lover looked at me and said,

"Sometimes, it's obvious you have never lost
someone." He, whose mother was taken from him
by her own body. He, who became one of those

parentless boys whose entire class showed up
for the funeral. This, which is not at all beautiful
nor poetic. Me, who still writes about it, who

gasps at death's sleight of hand, not knowing
how the trick actually works: no trap door,
no encore, no white dove buried up a sleeve.

Is empathy just a pretty mask for privilege?
One day, my father will die and I will be lucky
that it wasn't today. Perhaps then I will stop

writing these poems, no longer a weeping tourist,
a trite spectator caught between the glory of *god
is real* and *god is not real because if he was, if he was.*

## THE ORIGIN OF THE HEART AS
## AN INDICATOR OF LOVE

Sylvia Plath sat down at her kitchen table

and began to cut the beets into neat,
equal pieces. Their juice, a bottomless

pink, spilled out eagerly—each vegetable

a blood-heavy sponge. When she finished,
she wiped her hands on the front of her blouse,

smearing a cave painting across her chest.

Ted came home just as she was turning on
the oven. He saw the stain first, then her face,

pressed his fingers against the redness

and said *I want to be here.* He smelled
of unfamiliar perfume but she didn't care.

That man had looked right at her and said

he wanted to be right there: in the fluttering,
in the birdcage, against the ringing bell.

That night, they made love like two cadavers

reorganizing their organs. Later, while he
snored, the other woman's teeth still rattling

in his throat, Sylvia wrote in her journal:

*I have found it—the source of all my trouble,*
*the maker of all the racket. This bloody maraca.*

*This wild polygraph. It must know my truth.*

*I just need to listen. Listen. And yet? All I hear*
*is the endless procession, the pounding voice:*

*stay go / stay go / stay go*

## Without

There is a stage in early childhood development
when a baby realizes for the first time that
he is not, in fact, part of his mother's body.
That their heartbeats don't float together

down the river of her arm or pass each other
like corresponding voices along telephone wires.
One day, when she leaves the room, the baby
will comprehend that he is actually alone.

Such a heavy thought for something so small.
And, yes, perhaps it is strange to describe
myself as your child. It is problematic
to compare you—once my lover—to

my mother. You, who have painted my body
with your body. You, who startled the crows
of my heart. You are not my mother but
we did live inside each other for months.

It is the only adequate way I found to describe it.
One day, long after you left, I finally realized
you were actually gone. The suddenness.
The spark. Learning a new word for *without*.

## SMALL POEM

My sister is sick. Her belly is a flat lake.
Her mind is wrapped in a blanket of thistles.
I try to tell her it isn't the engine's fault
when the car doesn't start. She doesn't listen.

Her mind is wrapping a blanket of thistles
over her body, the small bird of her neck.
When the car doesn't start correctly, we listen
to it cough and heave itself into the toilet.

Her body is the smallest bird. Her neck
peels itself open (when she is too much)
to cough and heave herself into the toilet.
I do not want to write her as a sieve,

who peels herself open, who is never enough.
But she is disappearing before my eyes.
I do not want to write this. To sieve
my sister into a poem so small

but she is disappearing before my eyes.
My sister is sick. Her belly is a flat lake.
My sister is turning into the smallest poem.
She tells me it's the engine's fault.

# I HAVE MISTAKEN MYSELF

On the flight home, I cry
over a man who does not
love me. There is no stopping

the tears that flock to my ache
like needy children. The first,
the boldest, comes with

no warning just as the engine
begins its yearning howl.
Just as the plane's nose

abandons the earth to point
itself upward to face God,
or nothingness, which is

to say love. I pretend I am
just afraid of heights when
the attendant's eyebrows

pout with false concern:
*Is this your first time flying?*
I have carried too many

men around. *Would you
like a glass of water?* I have
mistaken myself for a bowl

of diamonds. *Don't worry
dear. It will be over soon.*
Really, who could love

an ox? Spent and blistered,
always dragging this bloody
plow. Listen to it scrape across

the pavement. Look at all
the land I've tilled. Look at all
the shit I could bury him in.

## SEVEN LAYERS OF HELL

In this room, a thousand
newborn mosquitoes.

In this room, Frida Kahlo
serves dinner to a crowd
of laughing white men
on her hands and knees.

In this room, every person
I ever regret fucking and
the sound of their orgasm.

In this room, the best
minds of my generation,
endless amounts of whiskey
and rope, one shotgun,
hundreds of bullets.

In this room, no matter
how hard I try, I cannot
remember your name.

In this room, every picture
is hung crookedly
and out of reach.

In this room, the baby
we never had is crying.

## Uninhabitable

My father still lives in the house he built
for my mother. He calls himself a bachelor,

not a hoarder, but you can measure how long
she's been gone by the piles of expired

mail, the dishes, the sun-stained photos
framed in dust—tree rings of his solitude.

When he speaks of his recovery, he lowers
his voice, even though we are on the phone.

He tells me he isn't ashamed of what he did
or where he has been or what he put my mother

through, but I think he means that he does
not allow himself the luxury of forgetting.

:::

I am writing about you again today and
I wonder, why dig up our sad corpse?

Why put the spleen back, a spoiled balloon,
already burst, but here I am huffing life back

into it. Nursing our fruitless love. Sometimes,
I still can't believe it. That you happened

and I happened and this was the best we could
do. Our nest of rubbish, our flowerless

garden—we slept here. Made love among
the bottle caps and ants and mold.

:::

My father told me he still imagines
getting back together with my mother,

maybe someday, after her new husband dies.
I think he means he started to build a house

and left it unfinished. What is it about
this family that draws us back to

the uninhabitable? That compels us
to make a bed where there isn't one?

# A BEEHIVE
# PITCHED
# IN THE RIVER

## THE LIVING ROOM NEEDS
## A NEW COAT OF PAINT

When I asked for it, you built a sturdy table
for our kitchen, even though it was summer
and you had to work outside with the mosquitoes.
You sanded down all the sharp edges, stained
its thick legs. You tuned each ivory tooth
of that old piano we found on the side
of the road. You tightened the fan above
our bed, the one that used to wobble,
seasick, like a drunk. You unclogged
the shower drain, fished out a month
of my hair. You are always fixing things.
But what is this, my love? A crack
in the ceiling. A faulty pilot light.
A keyhole in my sternum that opens
to an ocean of doubt. I stared into
your chest last night as if it were
a telescope. I saw our future
in the distance, an island
I will not swim to. I have
eaten my own legs.
I have cut my own
stitches. My love:
you cannot fix
what wants
to be bro-
ken.

# The Origin of the Funeral Hat

Twice, Coretta King dreamt
of her husband's assassination.
In the first dream, she sat frozen

as a centerpiece. He calmly opened
his mouth to let the bullet in like
a newborn leaning into a nipple.

In the second, he was dancing
in an uncrossable ballroom
and she could only watch

as a hundred tiny metal fists beat
themselves against his impervious
chest. Both nights she woke

in a sweat, shook him, whispered
"Martin, Martin," the way she
used to when they first tried on

each other's bodies, until her
husband finally came back
from sleep. Coretta always knew

what was coming. She grew up
watching boys who looked
like her husband grow up into

dead things, knew it was only
a matter of time—but when that
time came, all the fear left her body

like a procession. She wore a tall,
thatched hat to the funeral, black
as a crow's beak, and a veil circling

her face like an astronaut's helmet
as if to say, *I am not of this, I am only
a visitor.* As if to say, *if you're coming*

*for me too, then don't you dare miss.*
*Change, it moves like a bullet and*
*you already pulled the trigger.*

# For My Niece Livia, Age 8

*After Amy Gerstler*


It is 90° in Los Angeles this morning
and I am drinking hot mint tea. So much,
in fact, I have probably peed at least six times

in the past two hours. My voice is sore
and not ready to face the day. My throat
is a field, a cavern, a hill up which

a hundred words crawl. Sometimes,
it acts more like a waterslide—thoughts
running to the top only to slip back down

on their bellies. Livia, I realized this morning
that one day soon you will be old enough
to read my poetry. A scary thought

for your parents but no more alarming
than the fact that soon, your child body
will swell and stretch like an unfamiliar

dress, a building uncollapsing. Soon,
you will realize that everyone in the world
is afraid of looking stupid, and therefore,

you too will become afraid of looking stupid.
I want you to know it wasn't always like this.
Once, you entered the bathroom while

I was brushing my teeth. Mid-conversation,
you pulled down your pants and proceeded
to sit on the toilet, your tiny feet barely

brushing the tile floor. No pause. No
embarrassment. Quite literally business
as usual. You made soft grunting noises

as your body did what every body does.
I know that when you are old enough
to read my poetry and you find *this* poem,

the one about the sounds you made while
shitting, you will probably be embarrassed,
perhaps even hate me a little. I'm sorry.

Maybe it's the quirky aunt in me. Maybe
it's the poet who finds something thrilling
about unapologetic sounds, the dashing glory

of childhood that curdles at the arrival of shame.
How, in that moment, you reminded me of
my own animal, my heirloom fear of being

wild. How you, plank-legged fairy, princess
of wolves, have taught me to screech like
an owl or its witch. Livia, I am warming

my voice today and I feel like I am lacing up
my armor. I feel as though I am off to fight
the dragons or better yet, befriend them.

I am trying to teach poetry in school districts
that only know how to starve. I am trying
to show my students, who don't know

how to spell, how to write their lives
in anything but blood. I am trying to learn
how to give and foster forgiveness in a body

that wants none of it. When you are finally
old enough to read my poetry, I think
we will have a lot of catching up to do.

I have enjoyed relearning you as you age.
Every year unwraps a new layer. Every poem
is a different thread of me. Soon, you can

read each crude, screeching, slimy,
heart-wrecked line. My sweet firecracker.
My toothy walnut. Your mother has already

given you a bookish vocabulary, which
includes words like *feeble*, *specific*, and *galactic*—
abnormally large for the average 8-year-old.

Livia, your words are weapons; your voice
is the strength it takes to wield them.
Better yet, let's free ourselves of violence

as you have only ever been a valiant
champion of tenderness. Livia, your words
are lightning bugs. Your voice is the darkness

that allows them to glow. Please know
every sound you have ever made and will
ever make will always lead to grace.

So, until then, until we can swap poems
and cartons of ice cream, I leave you this note:
I am thinking of you on this scalding day

as I drink my tea. I am imagining your skinny
legs and your simmering laugh and your bursting
eyes and the way you climb confidently into

my lap to snuggle with your aunt, even though
you are getting so big and so wise and so soon,
you will be old enough to read all this.

## A Thousand Pieces

My mother does not write in her diary,
too afraid someone will read it. Instead,

she writes on scrap paper, rips it up
into a thousand pieces, throws it away.

  Once

my husband              slammed

            a thousand pieces
                        the screen door

the house      thousand shook

    pieces   fell off              I shook—my children

        are the only      pieces      things

keeping        from killing falling

                a thousand   into

pieces                                        my daughter is

            stubborn            like
            the dishes

I can't
            broke
                    the      thousand
                            pieces


        leave.

## PROGRESS REPORT

*A found poem from an e-mail written by my grandmother.*


He is in a wheelchair and
is pushed wherever he needs
to go. He no longer gets

physical therapy but they
walk him if he wants to.
It takes two people to walk

with him. He has been
eating quite well on thickened
liquids and mechanical foods.

Their goal is for him to
gain weight—has gained
two pounds since being there.

He participates in the activities,
especially the musical concerts.
He has not been roaming at night—

that phase of dementia is over.
It's okay to bring him candy.
We have been bringing

peanut butter cups (a favorite)
but I suspect anything sweet
is good. When Cindy visited,

he responded with "yes"
or "no" answers. He didn't
remember Julie was there

yesterday with her new dog.
He thinks he's in a hotel
and that's alright. He holds

tightly to our hands when
we say "good-bye" but doesn't
try to stop us from leaving.

# IN THE TRAIN STATION IN MUNICH

The train is late, a woman says to me, except
it is in German so I just smile a confused smile.

*I am sorry—I only speak English.* Her face round
as a pastry and dark as molasses or something

that isn't edible but still illustrates how she differs
from me without making her consumable.

It is cold here in Munich today, she says,
and she wouldn't normally take the train

but she doesn't feel like walking. Originally
from Ghana, her accent wraps each word

in a thick, wool blanket, her English stuffy
but warm. She tells me her daughter jumped

from the highest building in Las Vegas. No,
not suicide, she says, she was tied to a rope

and bounced right back up as if the earth
rejected her. Language is the passing of water

from hand to cupped hands. Impossible
not to spill, we lick the bounty off our wrists.

*But I could never come to America*, she says.
*Your police, they are too aggressive.* I imagine

the boy, the child playing with a toy gun—cowboys
and Indians, the game every white child gets to play

without being actually scalped or shot. I think
of the unarmed dead. I think of the families.

To hear a mother howling is to believe all humans
are animals and all animals are built to grieve.

*No, I do not want to come to your country. I tell*
*all my family in America, do not resist the police.*

*Do not question. Do not reach for your wallet.* It is
the only place where your money is no good.

# Thanksgiving, 2011

As we began our drive home
from Iowa, up the long sigh
of the Midwest, full of turkey
and the kind of fruit salad
that's made with Jell-O, talking
aimlessly about the desserts,
the tacky upholstery, I did not
expect you to turn off the narrow
road onto scattered gravel,
the parking lot of the graveyard
sagging out like the bounty
of a cornucopia. It would
sound too cliché to write
how the trees slouched just so,
the stone stumps like corn
scattered by some forgotten
god, the green green grass.
When I realized where we were,
where you brought me with
no warning, like death, my tears
came instantly—not because
you learned too young what a body
diluted looks like but because
I knew this was the moment
I would meet your mother, or
at least, where you lost her for
the last time. Back to the earth:
the farmer's wife, who bore land
and harvest and six strong sons
before that last, long winter.

# God Bless Your Fingers

Ten sugar-dipped strawberries. Ten humming sailors. Let the church say *amen*. Let the chapel doors open and open again. Ten gentle explorers who found my body buried inside itself. Who can see in the dark. Who can baptize me from across the continent. Let the church of my legs say *bless*. Let the church of my breasts say *oh god*. You have found the presents I hid from you. You have grown in me a basin I can never fill. Ten wise men. Ten pilgrimages across my stomach. Ten lit candles. Ten holy ghosts. I am a séance. I am a séance.

# Your Love Finds Its Way Back

One day, it just showed up on my doorstep.
Honestly, I don't know how it found me again.

The last night we spent together, I lured it

away with a trail of breadcrumbs—a necklace
swallowed one pearl at a time. Such a hungry

little bloodhound. I led it deep into the forest,

fastened its legs with twine. Dug a hole.
Said I *will jump if you jump* and it did,

just like I knew it would. And now,

here it is again—on its submissive back,
its pink underbelly exposed and I cannot say

I didn't want this. That I haven't waited

by the window. I sculpted your body
from the dust on the doorknob. I've hoarded

your name in my mouth for months. My throat

is a beehive pitched in the river. Look!
Look how long this love can hold its breath.

## MISSOURI

The man next to me on the train
smells like cigarettes. Not just one.
He smells like twenty years of smoke
in a house with no windows. I don't
normally talk to strangers but for some
reason, I ask him where he is going.
Missouri. His mother's house. Divorce.
Says she never treated the kids right.
Asks me what kind of woman ain't
meant to be a mother? He speaks like
he is unraveling a scroll in his mouth.
The flat body of Illinois floats past us
as if we were underwater. The train
becomes an eel drawing itself across
the bottom of the sea. We talk about
traveling. About the four states he has
yet to see: Alaska, Hawaii, Washington,
California. I tell him I'm sorry for
his unhappiness. He says he isn't
and I shouldn't be either. Just another
ride that's taking too long and it's time
for him to get off. In Missouri. Missouri.
He says it twice. Lets the taste of it
simmer in his mouth. Misery, he says.
Huh. Never realized it sounds the same.

# Remember

*This is your wife, Barbara.*

*This is your son, Scott.*

*This is you, in your Navy uniform,*
*waiting for the train to come.*

*You always said you only chose*
*the Navy because the uniform*
*matched your eyes. Remember?*

My grandfather coughs. I hand him
a water bottle. For the past hour,
we have been alternating between
a photo album and me reading
aloud to him from his 400-page
self-published autobiography.

When he fumbles, I open the bottle for him.
Our hands touch and his cloudy eyes
look up at me, wet with recognition.

The first page of the album contains
a note from the nursing home staff.
In big kindergarten letters, it reads:
You have a disease that affects
your memory. We are here to help.

*Look, Grandpa, this is the house*
*you grew up in. The farm.*
*You told me your sisters used to*
*put on extra layers before milking*
*the cows in the morning so the smell*
*of manure wouldn't follow them to school.*
*Do you remember your sisters?*

His words come out like shy children,
slow and hesitant. He tells me
he remembers but does not say more.

I read somewhere that people
with dementia might lie or pretend
to understand to avoid embarrassment.
I try not to think about this
and turn the page.

*This is you and Grandma*
*playing guitar. You always said*
*that she played bad and you*
*played worse. I remember when*
*you taught me my first chord.*
*It was the G chord. Remember?*

The bathtub is slowly draining.
The photograph is developing in reverse.
All those words just floating about.
His mouth an empty mason jar.
The fireflies just out of reach.

My grandfather picks up his autobiography,
holds it up in awe as if handing it to God
and says the most words he has said all day:
*Did I actually write this? I don't remember.*

If dementia is the body's longest goodbye,
then let these be the last memories
it pries from your fingers:

*This is your wife, Barbara.*
*You told me the summer you eloped,*
*her skin was sunburned the color of a cherry.*

*This is your son, Scott.*
*He has your eyes, navy blue.*
*This is the house you grew up in.*
*This is you, teaching. You were*
*a teacher. This is your wife singing.*

*This is your granddaughter.*
*She wants to be a teacher like you.*
*This is you. This is it. In the end,*
*this is all that is left.*

The memories, the moments, the people
who love you to the body's unflattering end.

Just yesterday, it seems,
you were waiting for that train.
It's here, Grandpa. It finally came.

# PAY THE BOATMAN

## Happy New Year

If the entire existence of the Earth—

all 4.54 billion years—were condensed
into just one year, accordioned together

like a head-on collision, humans

would enter the party in the second
half of the last minute of the last day.

Just in time to fall in love with

a stranger and coax the ball to drop
like a disco egg and spill out a fetal

new year. By then, the dinosaurs

would all be asleep, black-out drunk
from their 30-minute binge.

Imagine a world war that lasts

a heartbeat. A century passed over
like a page in a flipbook. A baby

conceived and buried as an old man

in the same moment. You and I
are not dinosaurs and we are not

buried yet, so think of your heartache—

the one festering inside you at this
very moment, the poison doe

nuzzling itself against your throat.

Picture your anxiety, your midnight
panic, your fear, your perennial doubt:

each of these becomes not even a word

in the book, barely a grain of sugar
in the bowl. This is not a devaluing

of your pain but a dethroning.

An adjustment of the microscope's lens.
Look up. The fireworks have started.

Kiss me. They will be gone so soon.

## A Stranger Died in an Avalanche

The angry manner in which
God wiped this one away—

like dust atop a piano, one petal

out of place in a still life. I picture
not his body but the flowers

shoved like rush hour passengers

into his mother's hands. His mother,
who is not a widow now but not

unlike one, the way childbirth

is a bodily vow. Why do we give
flowers to those closest to death?

White lilies are beautiful, yes,

with their blank faces, their sad
necks, but his mother will not

need more reminders of wilting.

I do not know this woman. I did
not know her son. He loved

someone I love and that is all. Death

twice-removed is a curious event.
Not as paralyzing as our house

on fire; not so far off that we can't

smell the smoke. I think of books
left unread, mornings spent not in love,

bodies choosing not to touch.

And if it is possible, I am thankful
for death because I am thankful

for life, because I can smell coffee

brewing, I can feel my mother
brush hair from my face, I can

lay lilies on her kitchen table.

# THE ORIGIN OF BREAST MILK

It began after the rape of St. Agatha,
a woman of God imprisoned in a brothel
for a month for rejecting a suitor.

She did not cry, even as
the shade was drawn on the first night
and the worst, most tired
parts of men found
themselves at her bedroom door.

Her first lover was a boy,
no older than fourteen.
Her second, a blacksmith.
Her third tasted like wet stone
and looked like her brother.
Her fourth, a drunkard, a widower.

In the morning, while Agatha slept,
women throughout Sicily
suddenly dropped their baskets of fruit
and pots of boiling water, their hands
grasping their chests—a wetness,

spilling, soaking through
every blouse. The doctors were called,
even the midwives. Women
began fastening cloth
around their torsos with twine.

Months later, months after
Agatha's breasts were cut off,
one woman weary with a colicky babe
untied the twine, pushed
the angry mouth to her nipple.

The child coughed at first,
then quieted, and it was all
so familiar. It was the way
it had always been but gentler,
the taking, the giving.

## Beautiful

It has become a struggle to get dressed
in the morning without hating yourself.

In the mirror, you see a sack of fruit,
a loveseat dragged to the curb. You know

this is not true. You know this is the plight
of those with mirrors and cloth and legs—

yet, still, you do not want to leave
the house. It is spring and you are dough

before the kneading. The man who
loves you from across the country tells you

your body is his home but you do not want
to believe him because why would anyone

want to live in a sand dune. He is a tourist
in a warring city. He only sees it when

the lights are on, before the shadows spill
like blood into the streets. Do not leave

the house. Do not even open your doors
when he comes knocking knocking

knocking with those words that can
make you feel but can never make you be.

# TEETH

The woman I am tutoring at the adult
ESL learning center has a tiny diamond

in the middle of her tooth. Technically,
it is her lateral incisor. I know this

from the hours I've spent at the dentist,
staring at the charts, memorizing

a family tree of gnawing to distract
myself from the stranger's hand

crawling inside my mouth which, I tell
myself, feels nothing like drowning.

I lie to this woman now, too. We are
practicing English sentences: useful ones

like *I would like to buy two please*
and *yes, I love America*. Her hijab

smells saccharine. Her henna-dipped
fingernails, like cuspids, bite into

her pencil. We read a story about a man
who works as a truck driver. We read

a story about a sick boy who needs
to lie down. I ask if she understands

the word *cushion*. She says *yes, to be*
*careful*. We read a story about a lion.

I ask if she knows the word *prey*. She says
*yes, Allah*, and points to the ceiling.

I try to explain how two words can look
different but sound the same. I wonder

if she, too, feels as though she is suffocating
with a stranger's hand pushing a brand new

shiny tongue into her throat. She smiles
and her lips pull back the curtain

to reveal her tiny, pin-sized star.
She asks me if I pray and I say yes.

## Exodus 33:20

When he doesn't want to look at it,

to rest his cheek against my thigh
and peer into the pink tender,

to examine where my body

becomes and unbecomes itself,
I can only assume that it is true

what they say about God:

it is impossible for man to look
upon the face of the sublime

and not be ruined by it.

The splendor would be insufferable.
How soft and quiet it is, where

the world begins.

## ODE TO MY BOTTOM LIP

You fat little worm.
You perch for a bird
to shit on. You child's face.
You slug of lust. I used to
hate the way you protrude
from my silhouette, elbowing
your way to the front
of the photo. How you always
betray my sadness, drag it
quivering to the surface
like a newborn seal. O tongue
dance partner. O kiss or leaf
blower. You have carried
my worst and best poems
to the world. You have tasted
the darkest parts of bedfellows,
blood and salt, and you
have hungered for both.
You swollen rooftop.
You waterbed of mouth.
I'm sorry I never saw you
for what you are: a cliff
words hurl themselves off.
A ledge lovers hang from.

# I Was Asked to Speak at Your Wedding

When I stand to give my speech,
everyone at the reception stares blankly
at my exposed shoulder. I notice
a barnacle the size of a teacup
growing from my collarbone.

Bundles of fish hang from
the chandeliers like metallic
earrings. I can smell their death
like fresh-cut grass. When I try to
say how happy I am for both of you,

minnows spill from my mouth,
hundreds of slippery lies, slapping
wet and hard against the banquet
table. I sit, ashamed of the mess
I've made. *Stupid animal*:

his hands, nothing like fins.
Someone hands me a conch shell.
When I hold it to my ear, I can
hear your lovemaking, the sound
of your bodies breaking.

## GARDENER'S DAUGHTER

Blackberry briar. Hunter's
daughter. Ocean-eyed mermaid.
When my sister needs to talk,

I extend my arms toward her
like a child asking to be held.
I turn my palms upward

as if donating blood and let her
empty the contents of the day
on me. Her words file out,

orderly at first and then a swarm,
spilling over me like the soft
swell of a mushroom cloud

until I do not remember where
I begin and her need ends. Once,
I held a newborn baby

in my arms—three weeks old,
naked as truth comes. She felt
so small. Her heartbeat: a moth

I trapped between my palms.
This is how to love the healing.
If my sister's eating disorder

were a person, it would be
a teenager by now. I imagine it:
doorknobs for knees, long

graceful fingers like the legs
of ballerinas, the beaks of cranes.
It would have a favorite book.

A locker combination. A best friend:
her. I tell her I won't let her live
in my house if she lets it sleep over.

I tell her I can't see it
but I know it's there. I tell her
nothing and just let the cloud

of her day rise like dough.
Milkweed woman. Catacomb
breast. This is how to love

the healing. To be not the sound
but the receptacle. To be not
the therapist, but the stop after.

To be not the paint, not the blank
canvas, not even the sweat
of creativity but to be the bed

the artist crawls back to. Tonight,
I rub my sister's shoulders. My thumbs
mistake her back for the staircase

in our childhood home. She tells me
she is scared, that the waves
are rising and the ship is begging

to become driftwood. The hounds
are howling tonight and the moon
is so full it could burst. She tells me

she has been symptom-free
for three weeks. Three weeks. It feels
so small. A newborn. A whisper.

A fluttering of smothered wings.
But sister, this is what it's like
to heal. To get up again and again

after the waves come. To retrain
the hounds of your body. Dragonfly.
Child of stone and moss. You are

dancing this dance you know
by heart. You are crawling out
from under yourself. Spring drinker.

Sap collector. You are drawing
a map to forgiveness, where you live,
where you already are—you just don't

know it yet. Perfect isn't where
we're from and we wouldn't like it
there anyway. Big sister. Little Dipper.

Who taught me how to sing
the way light streams through
a window. How to live boldy

and without shame. Sister,
when we were little, I didn't know
what it was like to face the dark,

twisting woods behind our house
alone. Sweet sapling. Falcon of
a woman. When I think of what

courage is, I see your hand
reaching back, leading me into
the forest, into the unknown.

The seam of your shoulder,
the horizon of your voice, saying,
"Look. I've got you. I'm here."

Blackberry briar. Gardener's
daughter. You were made to walk
through this. You were born

to travel that long journey into
yourself. Look into the distance.
I'm there if you need me.

Arms out. Ready to listen.
Ready to sing. Sweet sister,
I've got you. I'm here.

# TELEPHONE

When I ask if you have fallen
out of love with me and you

do not answer, I picture you
holding a tin can up to your ear.

I imagine a string tied
to its middle, like a leash

around the belly of a fat
silver worm. The string,

an escaped vein, runs down
your arm, over your knees,

along the bed, up my chest
and into my skin like a fish

hook or a feeding tube
threaded between the bars

of the birdcage around my heart.
I wonder if, when sketching

the rough draft of the body,
the Designer was afraid

our lungs would be too much
like wings and float away.

# FLOATING

He finally passed and we were
grateful. The living crave clarity:

*Yes, I am alive. No, he is not.*
Dementia gives none of that.
It starves those who remain

dry on land. My grandfather
spent the past two years floating

in the river that divides this
world from the next. One by one,
we offered to pay the boatman

to oar him to the other shore.
*It's okay,* we'd whisper when

we thought no one could hear,
*you can go now.* As if death
was a secret he had been keeping

for years. What I wouldn't give
to see what he saw in those last

dream months, what images
kept him here, long after his body
was able to be a body: the cow's

udder in his mother's hands;
sunlight migrating down

my grandmother's sleeping body;
the soft, steady bleating of
a sheep giving birth.

## AFTER GOOGLING AFFIRMATIONS
## FOR ABUSE SURVIVORS

*You have a fundamental right to a nurturing*
> *environment.* Oh, what a home I have
> built in my skull. What a dark, feral
> forest. There is no furniture, no artisan
> humanity. No gentle place to undress
> my own thoughts.

*You are a valuable human.* I think about death
> too often. I eat peanut butter with my
> fingers. I pee in the shower. I am
> a mouthful. Not a swallow. Not a bird
> or a name gone sour in his mouth.

*If you allow yourself to be mistreated, you are*
> *teaching that it is okay for others to*
> *abuse you.* And look at this shining
> curriculum! The lessons I have been
> prepping for months! Now, class,
> take out your inner child. Tell her
> she is so selfish. Tell her she shouldn't
> have eaten the last of the truffles.
> Tell her to take a good long look
> at love: her father gripping the throat
> of the payphone.

*You cannot assume responsibility or accept*
> *blame for any abusive behavior.* I am
> so sorry so sorry sorry so sorry he is
> so sorry sorry sorry so so sorry again

and again the conductor lifts her baton
and the musicians tilt their horns and
the song begins again.

*You do not have to feel guilty for allowing others*
        *to take care of themselves.* But what
do I do with all this leftover love?
My hands were built for crawling on.
How do I write myself gently? How
do I not worship the shipwreck that
stranded me here?

*You are not a failure or less of a person because*
        *you make mistakes.* I am not a failure
or less of a person because I make
mistakes. I write this until my hand
becomes a beggar. I write this until
the words no longer sound like words,
only sounds, and I can believe them now.

*Your higher power is transforming your brokenness*
        *and gently carrying you from darkness*
        *into light.* I believe in gentleness. Lord,
I believe in light. I am my own higher
power. I will carry myself out.

# SOME INVISIBLE MACHINE

# It Rained for Two Days Straight

Yesterday, Ryan told me his grandfather was readmitted to the hospital. It was raining the way it rains in the movies, like whoever does the dishes left the faucet running, heavy drops polishing everything in the city dark. We ran from one drooling awning to the next, quicker, then slower, quicker, slower. If one had watched from the sky, our bodies would have looked like two small needles being pulsed forward by some invisible machine, stitching the streets together. Today, Patrick was left by a girl he did not love but did not not love. He told me it was impossible to imagine himself both alone and whole. It was still raining—the sky's silly metaphor for sadness, untimely, startling, the way it makes the whole world more honest. Death is like this, too. Heartache, also. The sudden absence of what was there but now not. I touched Patrick's shoulder, attempting to pass my human to his. I sent Ryan a poem. I cannot do more than this art of bearing witness, to be both the bucket and the mirror, to say, *yes, you are here but I am here also*, to say *you won't be here forever,* or to say nothing and just walk beside each other in the rain.

## Won't You Let Me?

I want to run two fingers up
    your shins like a houseguest
        checking a windowsill for dust.

To sit in the basket of your pelvis
    and let my back fall like a jackknife
        against you, stomach up, breasts

fanning out like two pressed flowers.
    Please, won't you let me guide
        your hands like a seeing-eye dog?

We can coo and pant like curious
    animals, a carousel of old parts.
        My body was meant to

take in your body. To take in breath
    until there is no more room for either
        and my lungs must overflow

and my legs must overflow
    and my eyes turn back and head
        for home. To simmer and cool.

To feel your heart slow like a dying
    clock. To watch the sweat dry up
        like a river bed. Please, won't you

let me? Won't you let me curl up
    and purr against your neck like a cat
        and sleep until dinner time?

## Thirteen Stanzas for Sarah Winchester
## Whom I Think I Understand

After she lost her baby, Sarah went a little mad.
I understand her: the heiress of a gunshot fortune.
A boarded-up head. Her heart: a room with no doors.
Her daughter lost in a cupboard she could not reach.

I understand you, Sarah of the gunshot fortune,
who could buy her baby anything except breath.
Lost her daughter in a closet. She could not reach
her, or find her, found a medium to channel her.

Sarah, who could buy another baby with breath,
but wanted her Annie, her blue-lipped lily.
Could not find her, found a medium to channel her.
Instead, an omen: those killed by a Winchester rifle—

not your Annie, not your blue-lipped lily—
these spirits will haunt you into the dirt.
The omen from those killed by a Winchester rifle
shrouded her last lucidity, a sparrow in a shoebox.

These spirits would haunt her into the dirt
so she hired every carpenter in the city to build
upon the last of her lucidity, sparrow in a shoebox,
to evade the bulleted ghost, the endless mirages.

Sarah hired every carpenter in the city to build
all day and all night on her swelling mansion.
To evade the ghosts, with rooms like mirages,
staircases that lead to nowhere, doors that don't open.

All day and all night, the mansion swelled:
38 years of building, nonstop, bottomless cabinets,
staircases that lead and follow, doors that open
with a thousand keys. A room with no exit.

38 years of building, nonstop, bottomless inheritance.
I recognize her grief; how she hid it, made herself
a thousand keyholes. A room with no exit.
She too was a ghost, a wanderer of walls.

I recognize her grief; how it was hidden inside her.
She demanded 13 rooms. Her will written in 13 parts.
We both became ghosts, among the wandering walls.
13 panes on each window. 13 crashing chandeliers.

13 rooms with 13 locks. Her will written in 13 parts.
Signed her name 13 times *Sarah Sarah Sarah Sarah*.
13 steps to each window. 13 crashing chandeliers.
*Sarah Sarah* another candle goes out *Sarah Sarah Sarah*.

Signed her name 13 times *Sarah Sarah Sarah Sarah*
roaming the hallways, whispering her baby back:
*Annie Annie* a candle goes out *Annie Annie Annie*.
Sarah, I lost myself once, like your Annie, your baby.

I let a man roam my hallways. See, my baby back then
had a hunger—loved like a snakebite and I let him.
I lost myself, Sarah, like your Annie, my baby
made me a labyrinth. I am still haunted by

his hunger, his snakebite love. Sarah, I let him.
After I lost myself, Sarah, I went a little mad.
Made myself a labyrinth. He haunts me still.
My boarded-up head. My heart: a room, no doors.

## This, Too, Is Not for You

Between 6 a.m. and awake, you dream

of your professor calmly explaining
how much she enjoys your poetry

while she slowly cuts off your finger.

You wake when the knife hits bone.
In the kitchen, you drink weak coffee

and chop onions for the omelets

with a dull knife. You crack one egg;
two yolks fall out. Two wet coins.

Plump golden eyes turned up at you.

Your grandmother told you once
this was a sign of good luck, but

she also kept a small bottle of holy

water on her dresser and would smear
the cross over your forehead when

you had a cold. You dump the egg(s)

down the kitchen sink. Outside,
the wind ties itself around your ankles.

The smell of mud. Dried worms

across the driveway. A deer carcass
on the road makes you think of him.

You wonder what makes you so

attracted to rot. By noon you haven't
said more than twelve words: *good*

*morning I no thank you don't love*

*I'm sorry well enough.* The dull sun
slowly disappears down the drain.

The birds sing and this, too, is not for you.

## MADE FOR BLOOD

I cannot tell if we are falling out of love
with each other, or if this is the love
they warned us of: the love that doesn't

trim its grievances into neat, pleasing
bushes but instead grows itself wild
as the jaguar. Raised in captivity, it will

realize one day it, too, is made for blood.
The love that will hack up the wet,
pink carcass of an argument months after

its neck was snapped and swallowed.
The petty love. The selfish love. The love
that will stop apologizing and start

admitting to Sundays spent masturbating
to the thought of other men's fingers,
the way her head tilts back as she laughs.

# ONE MORE THEORY ABOUT MONEY

*After Paul Guest*


That it is important.

That it will die like a fairy
if you do not believe in it.

That there is such a thing as
too much, like chocolate
or heroin. That it is both
stomachache and overdose.

That it is not what makes
the world go round but instead
what makes the world brutally
murder each other.

That it does this, not you.

That it is the second coming of Christ.
That it will come when it is called.

That it will fill you up
as it starves your neighbor.

That it grows as sweet
as a peach and ripens
and rots the same, like us.

That it is only paper.
That it cannot be burned.

## Existential Crisis Brought Forth by Complaining about My Boyfriend over a Basket of Cheese Curds

I complain to my best friend about
how my boyfriend is an emotional
robot. He is not, of course, a robot,
nor is he emotionless, but he *is*

incredibly calculated and analytical,
unable or unwilling to be emotionally
stimulated beyond the realm of happy
or full. I, on the other hand, feel

emotions in Technicolor. I emote
not unlike a blender on high with
no lid and lots and lots of ice.
My friend laughs, takes another

long sip from his Manhattan and says,
*no, if he was a robot, you could just
program him.* This is true—another
moment in my life when my friends

are accidentally staggering and it isn't
just the bourbon. In a few drinks,
I walk home alone in the almost
but not quite spring weather.

I can see my breath—an eager child
running into the road before me.
I watch it spill out and fade like
a carbon copy of my heartbeat.

I wonder if I am just programmed
this way: to unearth a body just after
burying it, to find happiness and then,
like a video game, start over. I mean

really, if either of us are robots,
it's probably me: the one who doesn't
get lost but drives until the gas runs out.
The one who doesn't feel pretty until

she is told she is pretty. In other words,
the one who doesn't go until she is told
to go. Who doesn't believe in God
but can't find her own remote.

The glitchy one. The skipping record.
I have made this mistake before.
I have looked into the face of love
and said *no, not now* but meant *yes,*

*please, today.* I have pushed love
into a mirror and blamed it for
shattering. This is what I think
about as I crawl slowly into bed

next to a very warm, very breathing
body. I curl myself under his arm
and fall asleep, listening to
the buzz of our machinery.

# The Origin of the Bathrobe

Queen Mary stopped bathing
after her first miscarriage. She refused
to change her bedding, damp
with the wetness of labor and loss.

It was a compromise, at least,
to air them out to dry. They hung
like huge watercolor paintings on the trees,
plumes of sweat, blood, the spill
of what did not come.

By her seventh, the chambermaids
began wrapping scented scarves
around their faces. The Queen's nightgown
now stuck to her belly and thighs,
stiff, more red than white.
She seemed always pregnant

and always not. The ladies-in-waiting
were not foolish. They understood.
If a man were to see the Queen, soiled,
pacing ghostlike, no woman

would wear the crown again.
The ladies pulled down the curtains
and bed canopy and measured their bodies
by lying like dead angels on the floor.

Twelve matching housecoats
adorned with pillow tassels
and petticoat lace. Twelve
matching housecoats strolling
through the garden. Under one,
a tapestry of grief.

# At the End of the Day, I Am an Animal

It's been years since I've dreamt

of your fingers. And yet, my want
comes back unbeckoned as we stand

on a street corner, waiting for the light.

I loved only the idea of you for so long,
I forgot you had skin. That pliable field,

your brawny pelt, your animal smell.

Now, when I picture you naked, I see
nothing. No lumbering stomach,

no cock, no thighs, no flood of hair.

Deprive a woman of water for too long
and she will stop believing in rivers.

Tonight, we rehash the many ways

we poisoned ourselves—how sad it is,
how you forgot my father's name,

how I will not mother your children.

This is a sick dance and we know it.
Our desires: cannibal at best.

At the end of the day, I am an animal—

but in the morning, before I pull on
my hide, fasten my hooves and my snout,

I want you to know I am a soft voice.

I am dust falling in sunlight. Our love
can still be what it was, or, better yet,

what it never was. The unanswered call.

The seed meant only to be a seed. The dream
you can't remember but know was warm.

# Facts Written from an Airplane

The Victorians treasured human hair
because it is the only soft part of the body
that remains after death. I shaved my legs
in your shower. I hid long strands of myself
in your pillowcases. That is all that is left.

:::

Thinking of someone else during sex
is a cardinal sin punishable by nothing.

:::

The heart is wanting. The heart is
a hungry gas tank. The heart
is perpetually two years old.
The heart is bad at sharing.

:::

When the teacher asks
what grade you think
you deserve, you will
always say B+.

:::

51% of Americans voted for Obama
because the night before the election,
he slow-danced with his wife and
kissed her forehead, and we all want

so badly to believe that they actually
fucking love each other.

::::

Writing a list of ways I could be better
and writing a suicide note are the same thing.

::::

The heart lives in a packed elevator.
It doesn't know what floor it's waiting for
but it wants it wants it wants to get off.

::::

The Victorians believe when you write
a poem from an airplane, that moment
becomes suspended in the sky forever,
like a ornament in God's mobile.

So now you know: somewhere between
Phoenix and Las Vegas, a thousand miles up,
there you are like a grocery list pinned to blue.

## Mantra to Overcome Depression

Vitamin D. Sunlight. Go
outside. Get a good night

of sleep. Not *too* good.

Not shades drawn forever
good. Not like you used to.

Open the windows.

Buy more houseplants.
Breathe. Meditate. One day,

you will no longer be

afraid of being alone
with your thoughts.

Exercise. Actually exercise

instead of just Googling it.
Eat well. Cook for yourself.

Organize your closet, the

garage. Drink plenty of
water and repeat after me:

*I am not a problem*

*to be solved.* Repeat after me:
*I am worthy I am worthy*

*I am neither the mistake nor*

*the punishment.* Forget to take
vitamins. Let the houseplant die.

Eat spoonfuls of peanut butter.

Shave your head. Forget
this poem. It doesn't matter.

There is no wrong way

to remember the grace of your
own body; no choice

that can unmake itself.

There is only now, here,
look: *you are already*

*forgiven.*

# SING TO ME THEN

## PRAYER: HOPE, SCREAMING

A poet with clipped silver hair and a long
     pink skirt speaks into the microphone.

Tells us, the audience, how hesitant she was
     when her daughter became pregnant

because she didn't want her grandchild born
     while the country was at war. She clears

her throat and says, "Now I realize all babies
     are born during wartime." Every mouth

in the auditorium falls slightly open like soft
     wet flowers, a bouquet thrown at the foot

of the podium. She continues with a poem
     and we listen without listening. We are

thinking of our children, born or not yet sculpted,
     and of our parents and the times of war

in which we became. Was it desperate fear that
     caused our parents to reach for each other

in the darkness and pull out a voice? Or were
     we created as an act of protest—our parents'

defiant song, their demonstration, their favorite
     prayer: hope, screaming.

# THE TWO POET-DAUGHTERS

I was compared to a dead woman

in Florida last night. Her father,
drunk, soaked in grief, told *my* father

that *his* daughter was once a poet too

and his daughter was once a daughter
before she opened her faucets

and let them run into the night.

He found her, you know, her body
a drought. A soundless cello.

Last night, the two poet-daughters

were summoned like a memory
to his mouth. *It's not fair, you know,*

he slurred, *why my girl and not yours?*

          ::::

In the room that doesn't exist, where
you and I are made of the same

matter, I am braiding your hair.

You are reading your poetry
and it is the first time I have cried

from the graceful audacity of words.

Your body is light, and by that I mean
actually glowing, like your skin

could fill a whole room or a keyhole

or waltz with dust beyond the curtains—
you tell me that is not my best metaphor

and I smile because I know you are right.

*It's okay though,* you say, *we will think
of a better one tomorrow.* We fall

asleep in each other's arms, as the sun

in the room that doesn't exist
slides down the end of the world.

Somewhere, our fathers are singing.

## THESE HOURS I HAVE NOT LOST
## BUT DO NOT REMEMBER

I have calculated the total number of hours
we spend sleeping beside each other in a week

and I wanted to tell you it could be considered
a full-time job. We could be eligible for healthcare
benefits, could probably even pay for a mortgage

by now. I remind myself of this, in daylight, when
I miss you and cannot reach across the bed

for the comforting filling and refilling
of your chest. Such a strange affair
we are having with each other; these hours

that I have not lost but do not remember.
This cannot be the best of love: to drool

on someone's collarbone or inhale an elbow
or be woken by the most ungraceful
sounds of the body. But what is it if not

the softening of grips? A letting go. Your heart
finally slowing that stubborn, lonely march.

## Today Means Amen

Dear you, whoever you are, however you got here,
this is exactly where you are supposed to be.

This moment has waited its whole life for you.
This moment is your lover and you are a soldier.

Come home, baby, it's over. You don't need
to suffer anymore. Dear you, this moment

is your surprise party. You are both hiding
in the dark and walking through the door.

This moment is a hallelujah. This moment
is your permission slip to finally open that love

letter you've been hiding from yourself,
the one you wrote when you were little

when you still danced like a sparkler at dusk.
Do you remember the moment you realized

*they* were watching? When you became
ashamed of how much light you were holding?

When you first learned how to unlove yourself?
Dear you, the word *today* means *amen*

in every language. Today, we made it. Today,
I'm going to love you. Today, I'm going

to love myself. Today, the boxcutter will rust
in the garbage. The noose will forget

how to hold you, today, today—
Dear you, and I have always meant you,

nothing would be the same if you
did not exist. You, whose voice is someone's

favorite voice, someone's favorite face
to wake up to. Nothing would be the same

if you did not exist. You, the teacher,
the starter's gun, the lantern in the night

who offers not a way home, but the courage
to travel farther into the dark. You, the lover,

who worships the taste of her body, who is
the largest tree ring in his heart, who does not

let fear ration your love. You, the friend,
the sacred chorus of *how can I help*.

You, who have felt more numb than holy,
more cracked than mosaic. Who have known

the tiles of a bathroom by heart, who have
forgotten what makes you worth it.

You, the forgiven, the forgiver, who belongs
right here in this moment. You, this clump

of cells, this happy explosion that happened
to start breathing, and by the grace of whatever

is up there, you got here. You made it
this whole way: through the nights

that swallowed you whole, the mornings
that arrived in pieces. The scabs, the gravel,

the doubt, the hurt, the hurt, the hurt
is over. Today, you made it. You made it.

You made it here.

## RELEASE IT

You are not the first to domesticate it.
Your shame: pretty as a house pet.
You bathe it nightly, comb its matted
carpet. When will you stop letting it

sleep in your bed? Some part of it
comforts you—that dank heaviness
curled at your feet like a bird's nest
of forks. When will you put it down?

End its reign, its gnarled suckling
of your last good teat? You, on
your knees, still. You, crawling out
of that man's mouth, still. Let go

of the fact that you were the other
woman once, twice. Lust spent like
inheritance does not define you.
Let go of being made of hunger: *yes,*

*I ate all six macaroons on the sparkling
streets of Budapest that night. I saved none
for you.* Sweetheart, shame has been
bound in your basement too long.

Release it. Your floorboards shudder
at the thought of your belly, smooth
as an apple, kissing flat against it.
Release it. Your hands are not

as small as they used to be. Get up.
This is not who you are anymore.
Worth is not a well to be poisoned.
It is not a tumbler being filled or

drank from by some audacious god,
nor a monthly allowance we get
when we are not not beautiful.
Drive to the ocean. No, drive to

the Redwoods. Drive to whatever
landmark most reminds you that
becoming is a slow glory and leave
your shame. It will not follow you home.

## TONIGHT IN YOGA

I realized I have been afraid of meditation
        my whole life, which is to say,

I have been afraid of myself my whole life,
        which is to say, my whole life

I have been afraid of the anti-silence
        of my thoughts, which is to say,

I have not been myself my whole life,
        which is to say *I'm sorry*, which is

to say my whole life has been *oh, I'm so
        sorry*, which is to say don't meditate,

just apologize—don't worry, just be
        worried all the time, every day

for your entire life that you, your heart,
        is broken, like an engine,

like a wine glass, like an oven you can't
        even stick your head in, it won't

work right, can't love right, but tonight
        in yoga, I realized for the first time

that breathing is not the process of being filled
        and emptied: breathing is the act

of actually making love to the whole world,
        which is to say the world is

your lover, which is to say love the whole
        world, in all its sweaty folds

and scabbed pockmarks, which is to say
        love your dirty corners, your

stalk-like legs and barrel hips, love all
        the no and the no and the no

that brought you right here, to this moment
        and love the yes. The yes:

the breath that found its way to you, built
        a home in your blood cells,

changed itself to better suit you and for it,
        tonight, you say: I was made to

breathe and move and give, which is to say
        love. Love. I was made to love.

# THE LUCKY GROW OLD

One day, we will look up from
our breakfast cereal and realize

our lives have slowly thinned

and lengthened like dough
rolled under our fingers. Time,

the coiling snake, the silent train.

We count the boxcars as it passes
and this makes us feel as though

we understand it. One day,

if we are lucky, our skin will
hammock and sag. Our voices

will dry up like wells. I hope

you will still sing to me then.
I hope we find our way together

across this knotted forest of time:

that strange witness, the faceless
map—*I know where I am going*

*but don't know what it looks like.*

One day, our love will shed
its skin for the hundredth time.

Touching will be a royal dance,

a séance of the tired, a ceremony
of seasons, constantly reborn

only to wither in your arms.

## The Day of the Last Fire

Volcanoes across the world coughed up
dark parts of the earth they swallowed

long ago. Aloe plants gave up and withered.
Matches were discontinued only to be

re-marketed as fat toothpicks. Fire trucks—
auctioned off in bulk as questionable

party buses and/or discount limousines.
Although it was predicted, scientists could

never explain why it happened. They blamed
climate change, the moon, the decline

of emotional intimacy in young people
these days. Families gathered around

the gas stove to watch water boil for
the last time. Smokey the Bear was fired.

Candles were lit—millions of them—
deathless vigils coddled like newborns.

Heavy breathing was made temporarily
illegal. The fireworks ran out surprisingly fast.

The world's supply only lasted four hours,
but in that time, it was like God let Pollock

into heaven's liquor cabinet. You built
a bonfire in the backyard from three-legged

chairs, egg cartons, and the dead Christmas
tree you dragged from the alley. I added

my worst poems, my journals from the years
I wrote only about drowning. You let me

light it and we watched that fucker burn
all night until ash fell hushed as snow

around us, till the crackle and hiss
of things disappearing quieted, then

stopped, until the fire was as small
and glowing as your hand in my lap.

## CHAI & WHISKEY

In the small claw-foot bathtub,
we drank cold chai and whiskey
and sat entwined like a car accident
or the way newborns instinctively
cling to anything. There were
candles and the last light from
the day's final drag home and
the water, so warm our skin
seemed to blend together.
*This must be real love,* I said in
the more poetic draft of my life.
In reality, we sat tangled until
our asses numbed and our joints
cried and we argued about money
and the dog and how you never
tell me I'm sexy until after you
pull out. But, this must be real
love though, right? Because
we stayed in that porcelain coffin
until the sun clocked out. Until
our toes and fingers sulked inside.
Because even after the water cooled
and emptied back into the ocean,
we still stayed—holding each other,
arguing, crumpled together in
that tub not meant for two or even
someone your size. Until the candles
burned out, until we were dry.

## about the author

Sierra DeMulder is an internationally touring performance poet and educator. She is a two-time National Poetry Slam champion, one of the founders of Button Poetry, and the author of *The Bones Below, New Shoes on a Dead Horse,* and *We Slept Here.* Sierra lives in Minneapolis with her dog, Fidelis.

## acknowledgments

I would like to extend all my gratitude to Grace Suh for finding and believing in me; Andrews McMeel for making this journey possible; Michael Mlekoday and Neil Hilborn for their talent and patience; Rya, Cheyenne, Brian, and Mom for being more than just family; the brilliant folks at Button Poetry; Claire Biggs and the entire crew from To Write Love on Her Arms; everyone who has graciously supported me over the past decade—you are why I am here today; and finally, my father, for being my loudest supporter and my greatest source of joy.